Rigby

Great Strides

Critical Thinking Skills

Rigby

A Harcourt Achieve Imprint

www.Rigby.com
1-800-531-5015

ACKNOWLEDGMENTS

STAFF CREDITS
Editorial: Vicky Aeschbacher, Heera Kang, Lori Najar, Tina Posner
Design: Amy Braden, Joan Cunningham, Joyce Spicer

ILLUSTRATIONS
P. 27 David Wysotski; p. 30 Ken Gamage; p. 36 Joe Kulka;
p. 42 Vincent Nguyen

PHOTOGRAPHY
P. 8 ©Jose Luis Pelaez, Inc./CORBIS; p. 9 ©DiMaggio/Kalish/CORBIS;
p. 14 ©Aurora/Getty Images; p. 15 ©George D. Lepp/CORBIS; p. 15
©Aurora/Getty Images; p. 20 ©Bruce Bennett Studios/Getty Images;
p. 21 ©Bruce Bennett/Getty Images; p. 46 ©Mark Peterson/CORBIS;
p. 47 ©Raghu Rai/Magnum Photos; p. 52 ©NASA/Photo Researchers,
Inc.; p. 58 ©Mark Peterson/CORBIS; p. 59 ©Otto Greule Jr./Getty
Images; p. 59 ©Icon SMI/CORBIS.

Additional photography by Photos.com Royalty Free and PhotoDisc/
Getty Images.

YOUNG ADULT WRITERS
P. 42 JoAnn Hernandez

ISBN 1-4189-2919-0

© 2007 Harcourt Achieve Inc.

Critical Thinking Skills help you to make decisions about what you read.

So you will be able to:

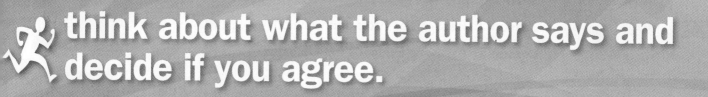

think about what the author says and decide if you agree.

question whether the author is fair or biased.

decide what's important to remember and use what you learn when reading more about that topic.

Table of Contents

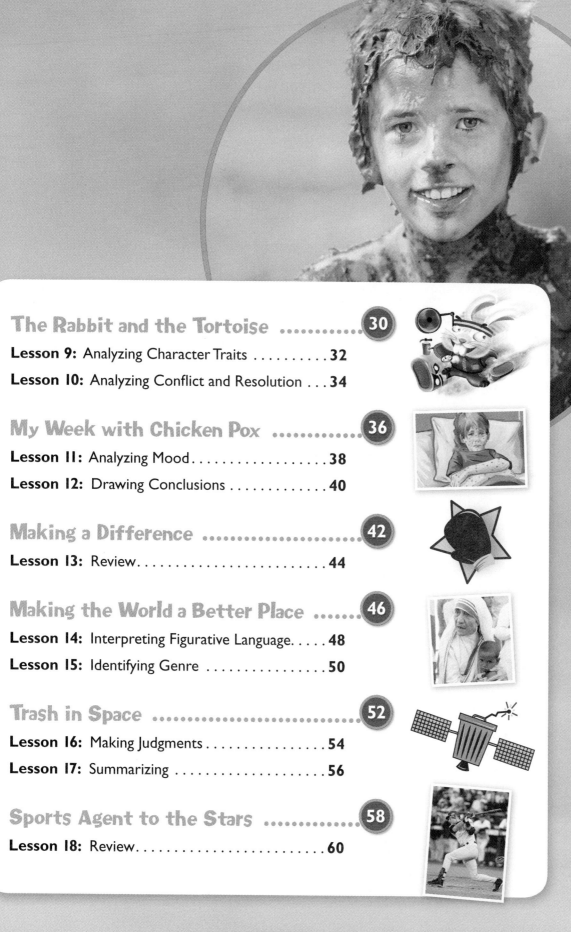

Critical Thinking Skills Roleplay

Student 1: The question asks us how the person who wrote this poem would feel about today's popular TV shows.

Student 2: They're really popular. It seems like everyone wants to be famous now.

Student 3: Well, it looks like the person who wrote this poem wasn't too interested in fame.

Student 1: Yeah, but her biography says that she turned out to be a really famous person.

Student 2: That happened after she died. She didn't try to be famous.

Student 3: Anyway, her poem says that it would be dreary. That means dull and depressing. So she's against fame.

Teacher: That's good thinking. See if you can figure out why she has this opinion of fame. That will help you answer the question.

Student 1: Well, she compares a famous person to a frog. I once saw a bullfrog all puffed up and looking very silly.

Student 2: Also, in the poem, the frogs are telling their names to an admiring bog. A bog is like a swamp.

Student 3: So to her, those people on TV might as well be frogs trying to get attention from a swamp. In other words, she'd probably think they were boring and silly for caring so much about fame.

Teacher: When you read, think about <u>what</u> the writer says and <u>how</u> the writer says it. That helps you understand the writer's viewpoint. Then decide if you agree. That's using critical thinking skills.

Your Turn

Read the list of tasks. Then sort them into the chart below. Remember, when you use critical thinking skills, you think about the reading in a more general way.

- Summarizing an article
- Listing events in the right order
- Deciding why the author wrote something
- Using story clues to predict what will happen next
- Deciding if school uniforms are a good idea
- Finding information on a chart or map

Critical Thinking Skills Are Good For	Critical Thinking Skills Are NOT Good For

Write Back...

The next time you need to make decisions about the information that you're reading, what will you do?

Don't Give Up Your COMPUTER

Computers are not just about games.

Comprehension Skills

- **Lesson 2:** Recognizing Facts and Opinions
- **Lesson 3:** Assessing Evidence for Opinions

Reading Strategy

Use Background Knowledge
Use what you already know to help you understand what you read.

Once upon a time there was no Internet and no video games. It's hard to believe. Today people spend a lot of time looking on the Internet and playing video games. Some people are concerned about kids who spend a lot of time on computers. They believe that kids will be better learners and better people if they give up their computers. That's just crazy. Kids need computers to learn to live in a modern world.

Let's face it. Kids spend a lot of time on their computers. Some spend up to 30 hours a week surfing the Internet. That *is* a lot. But kids are learning, too.

Students need computers for school. They use the Internet to find information for homework. Information does not just jump off the screen. It takes skill to figure out where to find the right information. E-mail is also useful. For example, what if you lose your homework assignment? You can e-mail a friend to get it quickly.

Many girls and boys spend up to 30 hours a week on the computer.

Is this more than just a game?

Some adults say video games are a waste of time. They think kids spend too much time playing them. In the United States, 64% of all children play video games at least one hour a day.

Other people say that video games are too violent. They see games in which players must kill to win. Not all video games are about killing. A growing number of games are about learning. Video games can help kids learn math, science, and even reading skills. Some **simulations** teach teens to drive cars, start their own businesses, and build healthy communities.

Many people are afraid that kids don't learn how to communicate with others when they spend so much time on computers. That is ridiculous! Today kids communicate with their friends through instant messaging. They can play **cooperative** games across the Web. In fact, computers are bringing people together across the whole world. Now a kid in Iowa can communicate with friends in Mexico, Iraq, and Germany all at once. Kids can even talk with experts such as astronauts or scientists. What could be more educational than that? ■

What Do You Think?

Do kids spend too much time on computers?

☐ Yes, they are wasting time.

☐ No, they are developing skills.

Vocabulary

simulations: situations similar to ones in the real world

cooperative: shared

Lesson
2 Recognizing Facts and Opinions

Your Turn

Reread the passage. Draw a line under facts and circle opinions. Then write them in the chart below.

Facts (statements you can prove)	**Opinions** (feelings and beliefs)

Your Choice

Circle the correct answer.

1 **The author believes that computers and video games are —**

    A. useless inventions.
    B. great tools for learning.
    C. bad for social skills.
    D. bad for young children.

2 **Which of the following is a fact about computers?**

    A. Students are not learning from computers.
    B. Computers are not good for students.
    C. Kids play games on computers.
    D. Computers help students to be healthy.

3 **Which of the following is an opinion about video games?**

    A. Once there were no video games.
    B. Video games keep score.
    C. Video games are a waste of time.
    D. Some video games are violent.

4 **Which kind of game is cooperative?**

    A. one that kids do alone on long trips
    B. one that kids play with friends
    C. one that kids use to learn math when they are home sick
    D. one that kids play when they need to be quiet and alone

(See answers for Critical Thinking Skills, Lesson 2 to check your work.)

Number Correct:

Write Back...

Why is it important to be able to recognize facts and opinions when you read?

Your Turn

Read the opinion in the top box. Reread the passage and circle three reasons the writer has this opinion. Then draw a line under evidence for the opinion. Fill in the chart with reasons and evidence. One has been done for you.

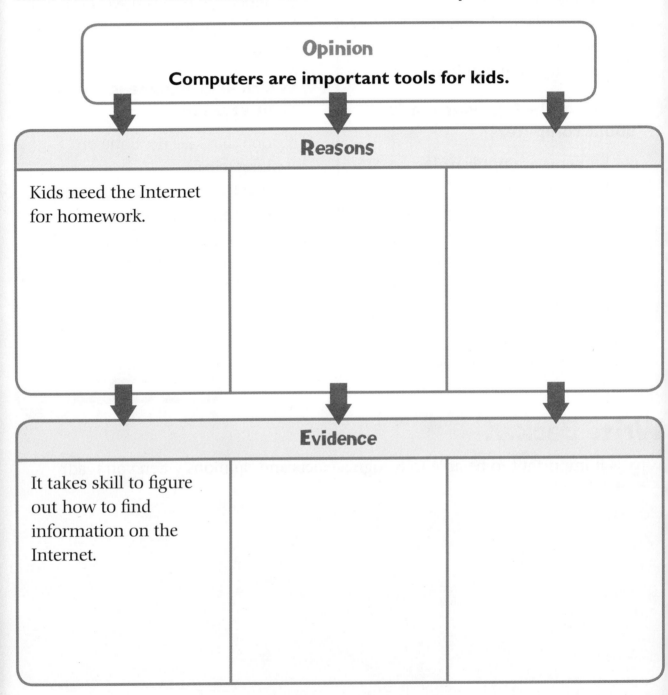

Opinion

Computers are important tools for kids.

Reasons

Kids need the Internet for homework.		

Evidence

It takes skill to figure out how to find information on the Internet.		

Your Choice

Circle the correct answer.

(1) How does the author feel about the Internet?

A. He or she thinks that it's dangerous.
B. He or she thinks it's really useful.
C. He or she has no feelings about it.
D. He or she hates it because it is difficult to use.

(2) Which of the following is evidence for the opinion, "Video games are a waste of time."?

A. All video games are too violent.
B. They help with information for homework.
C. They help young people figure out problems quickly.
D. 64% of all kids play video games at least one hour a day.

(3) Good evidence —

A. supports reasons.
B. is always interesting.
C. shows how a person feels about something.
D. gives an opinion.

(4) A simulation helps you learn by —

A. searching the Web.
B. e-mailing friends.
C. putting you in a real-world situation.
D. doing math, science and reading.

(See answers for Critical Thinking Skills, Lesson 3 to check your work.)

Number Correct:

Write Back...

How do reasons and facts help people accept an opinion?

Jump into Thin Air

Who needs an airplane for skydiving?

Reading Strategy

Stop and Think About What You Read
Often, readers rush through important details. Take a break as you read to make sure that you understand everything.

Would you be brave enough to jump off a high cliff? Would you leap from a tall bridge? Some people do. They, of course, wear parachutes. Actually, they use chutes called parafoils. This kind of chute is not round. It looks like a wing or a sail and allows jumpers to steer using wires from the edges.

Jumping from a tall place is called B.A.S.E. jumping. The letters stand for **B**uilding, **A**ntenna, **S**pan (bridges) and **E**arth (cliffs.) Jumpers don't use an airplane. They leap off a solid base into the air.

Jumpers have to be well trained to do this. Base-jumpers receive all kinds of instructions to get them ready to jump. They need to do hundreds of jumps from an airplane. Most jumpers are also strong athletes.

Many cliffs must be climbed first. That means jumpers also have to be able to **scale** mountains. They need to have quick reactions. They often have to make sudden movements. They also need to be strong mentally because, not surprisingly, humans have a natural fear of falling. **Conquering** fear gives people a feeling of power in addition to the excitement of the jump.

Base-jumpers have to open their parachutes before they near the ground.

How It All Began

People have been jumping into the air for a long time. Around 1600, a man was brave enough to jump off a tower with a parachute. He was the first B.A.S.E. jumper. In 1793, a hot air balloon exploded. The man inside was the first person to use a parachute in an emergency.

In 1911, the first skydivers jumped from an airplane on purpose. They jumped holding a folded parachute against their chests. By the 1960s, skydiving became popular. Now B.A.S.E. jumping is becoming popular, too. Would you dare jump into thin air? ■

Vocabulary

scale: to climb
conquering: overcoming, mastering, or beating

Free Fall

Is it a dream?
Falling, falling.
But it isn't a dream.
Falling, faster, falling.
I used to have my feet
On that ground.
Now it's just a little
Patch of color below.
Am I heading toward it?
Or is it flying up to meet me?
Now I shoot like an arrow
Ripping the silence into a roar
The chute opens, flapping
Like flags on a windy day
The earth bigger, bigger
I pull the ropes harder
And slide in. Safe!

A parafoil chute allows the jumper to steer clear of any objects on the way down.

4 Making Generalizations

Your Turn

Circle two ideas that are alike. Underline other ideas that are alike. Use what you've marked to fill in the chart below.

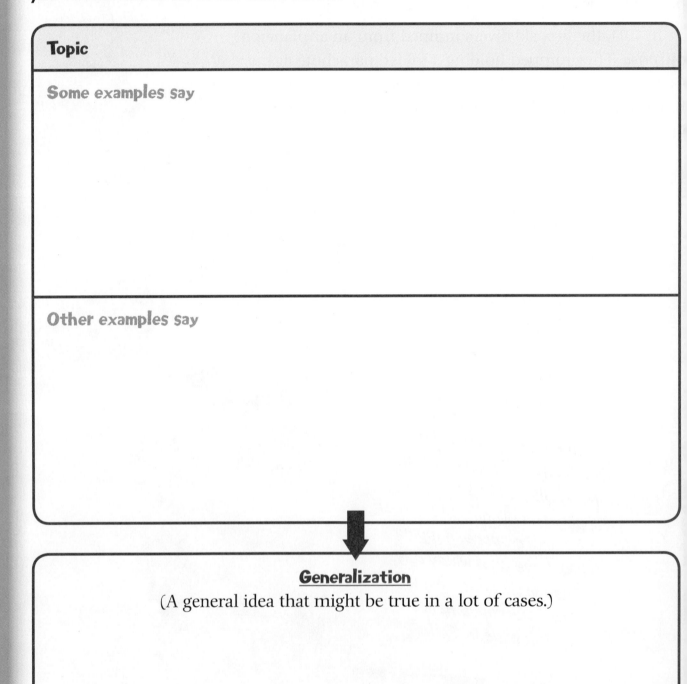

Topic

Some examples say

Other examples say

Generalization
(A general idea that might be true in a lot of cases.)

Your Choice

Circle the correct answer.

1 **B.A.S.E. jumpers leap from —**

   A. planes.

   B. high ground.

   C. balloons.

   D. army bases.

2 **What is generally true about B.A.S.E. jumping and skydiving?**

   A. Both need planes.

   B. Both need mountain climbing.

   C. Both need the same kind of parachute.

   D. Both need jumpers who can fight their fears.

3 **Getting the right equipment and a lot of practice are important for —**

   A. all B.A.S.E. jumpers and skydivers.

   B. B.A.S.E. jumpers only.

   C. skydivers only.

   D. only people jumping for the first time.

4 **Which of the following items might you scale? —**

   A. a balloon

   B. a ladder

   C. a parachute

   D. an airplane

(See answers for Critical Thinking Skills, Lesson 4 to check your work.)

Number Correct:

Write Back...

How does making a general statement about what you read help?

Connecting Across Texts

Your Turn

Go back and put a check mark next to ideas and details that both texts share. Write them in the space at the center of the chart. Write details that are different into the outside boxes.

Jump Into Thin Air

Details Both Texts Share

Free Fall

Your Choice

Circle the correct answer.

1 **What other sport is most like B.A.S.E. jumping?**

A. racecar driving
B. airplane flying
C. rock climbing
D. skydiving

2 **"Free Fall" helps a reader understand —**

A. how base-jumpers feel.
B. what base-jumping means.
C. the dangers base-jumpers face.
D. the order of developments.

3 **The article "Jump into Thin Air" gives —**

A. information about how jumpers feel.
B. information about what B.A.S.E. jumping is.
C. details about how to become a B.A.S.E. jumper.
D. a scary story about one B.A.S.E. jumper.

4 **When you conquer something you —**

A. hide under it.
B. give up doing it.
C. enjoy it.
D. beat it.

(See answers for Critical Thinking Skills, Lesson 5 to check your work.)

Number Correct:

Write Back...

How does thinking about the ideas in the two texts help you?

Wild About Hockey

About Hockey

Playing hockey was all Pat LaFontaine ever wanted

Reading Strategy

Question Yourself

As you read, ask yourself what the author is trying to do. Is he or she trying to convince you of something? How do you feel about what the author is trying to do?

Like a lot of kids, Pat LaFontaine loved hockey. He dreamed of playing in the Olympics and of playing **professionally**. Pat achieved his dreams at a young age, but then things went wrong. Pat's life changed in a big way. He lost his dream of a long career in hockey. He found an even better one though. His new dream has made him even more of a champ than ever.

In 1980, Pat was 15 years old. That year the U.S. hockey team won a gold medal in the Olympics. Pat dreamed of being one of those Olympic athletes. He left home when he was only 16 years old to move to Canada where he could train with Canadian athletes. There, Pat played on a junior hockey team.

Many people said Canadian hockey was too tough for a teenager from the United States. They were wrong. Pat led the **league** and broke many records. In 1983, Pat was named the best junior hockey player in Canada. He was excellent.

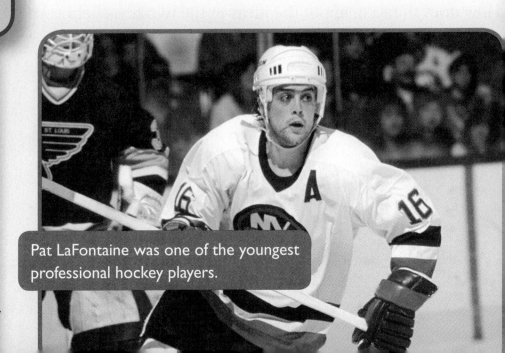

Pat LaFontaine was one of the youngest professional hockey players.

Pat was great at scoring goals!

In 1983, at age 18, Pat became a professional hockey player. The New York Islanders chose Pat for their team because he was a tough player. Pat was excited about playing. However, there was something else he had to do. Pat played on the 1984 U.S. Olympic hockey team. The team did not win any medals, but Pat scored many goals. Playing in the Olympics was the greatest feeling of all!

Pat played for the Islanders for many years. He was one of the team's best players. Unfortunately, in 1998, Pat had to quit. A head injury caused him to give up the sport he loved. Pat's injury took a long time to heal. He met a lot of kids while he was in the hospital. They had serious illnesses. Their stories helped Pat get better.

Today, Pat spends his time raising money to help sick kids. Not only was Pat a great athlete, but he is also a great human being. His power helping kids is even greater than his power on the ice. Pat should get a gold medal for **heroism**! ∎

Vocabulary

professionally: as a paid athlete
league: a group of teams that play against each other
heroism: being a hero

Recognizing Bias and Viewpoint

Your Turn

Reread "Wild About Hockey." Circle positive things the writer says about Pat. Underline negative things the writer says about Pat. Use this evidence to fill in the scale below. You can tell the author's bias by which side of the graphic organizer has more evidence.

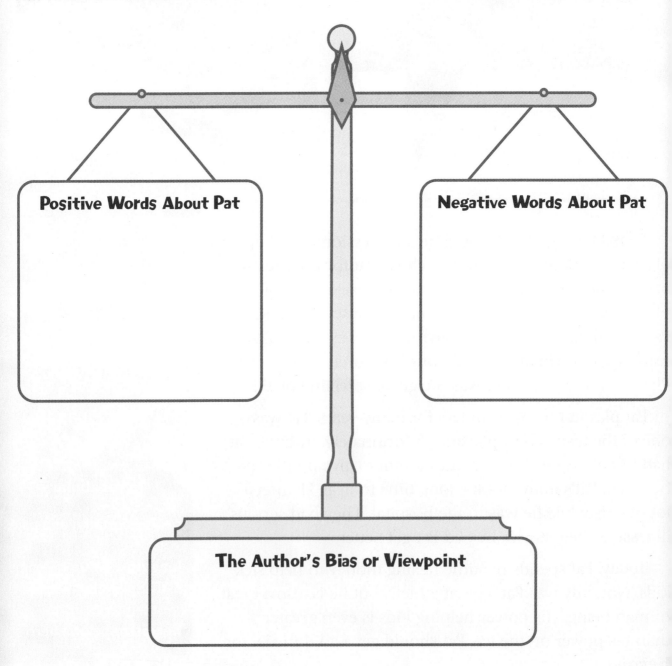

Positive Words About Pat

Negative Words About Pat

The Author's Bias or Viewpoint

Your Choice

Circle the correct answer.

1 **Why did Pat LaFontaine start raising money to help sick kids?**

A. Their stories had helped him get better.
B. It was his job.
C. He wanted them to learn how to play hockey.
D. He needed more fans.

2 **When a writer only presents one side of an issue, you can guess that the writer has a —**

A. setting.
B. bias.
C. problem.
D. dream.

3 **Which sentence from the passage shows that the writer admires Pat LaFontaine?**

A. In 1980, Pat was 15 years old.
B. Pat should get a gold medal for heroism!
C. Pat was excited about playing.
D. Pat played on the 1984 U.S. Olympic hockey team.

4 **Pat LaFontaine played professionally. In this sentence, *professionally* means —**

A. hockey.
B. quickly.
C. for attention.
D. for money.

(See answers for Critical Thinking Skills, Lesson 6 to check your work.)

Number Correct:

Write Back...

Why is it useful to know a writer's viewpoint?

Identifying an Author's Purpose

Your Turn

Read "Wild About Hockey" again. Circle facts and information. Underline the writer's arguments. Highlight ideas the writer uses to make the writing fun. Then, add these to the graphic organizer. What do you think is the author's purpose?

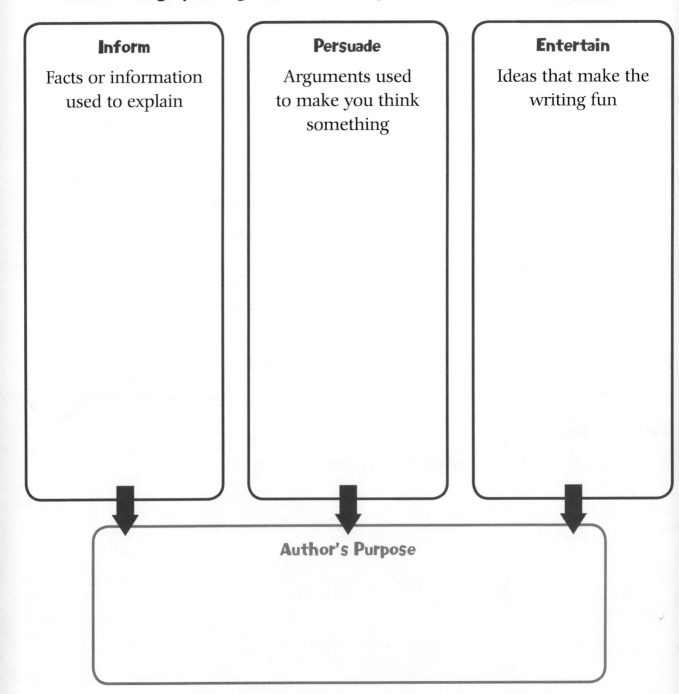

Inform

Facts or information used to explain

Persuade

Arguments used to make you think something

Entertain

Ideas that make the writing fun

Author's Purpose

Your Choice

Circle the correct answer.

1. **What caused Pat LaFontaine to give up playing hockey?**
   A. He forgot how to play.
   B. He was not good enough.
   C. He got a childhood disease.
   D. He had a head injury.

2. **Authors who want to inform must offer lots of —**
   A. ideas.
   B. opinions.
   C. facts.
   D. descriptions.

3. **The author wrote "Wild About Hockey" to —**
   A. persuade readers that Pat LaFontaine is a wonderful person.
   B. persuade readers to give money to help sick children.
   C. inform readers about Pat LaFontaine's injury.
   D. entertain readers with stories about Pat's childhood.

4. **Which of the following is an act of heroism?**
   A. pulling a person out of a car after a wreck
   B. fixing the tire on an old bicycle
   C. finishing homework late
   D. writing an essay about a famous person

(See answers for Critical Thinking Skills, Lesson 7 to check your work.)

Number Correct:

Write Back...

The next time you read something, how will you figure out the author's purpose? Why should you care?

The Smelly SWAMP THING

Is there a strange creature in the swamps of Florida?

A strange creature may live in Florida. It is said to be seven feet tall and look like a hairy ape. People say it smells awful, too. The smell is said to be like rotten eggs mixed with skunk spray. People call it a skunk ape.

The home of this smelly **primate** is supposed to be the Everglades. This very large area is mostly a swamp with lots of tall sea grass. More than a dozen **endangered** species of birds and other animals live in the area. It also has millions of bugs that keep people away for much of the year. The Everglades has many small islands, too. If the creature did live here, there is plenty of room to hide.

David Shealy claims to have seen the skunk ape. He says he first saw it more than 30 years ago when he was a kid. He was out in the swamp when he smelled something terrible. He went home, but much later he came back with a camera and took a picture.

Some people think the skunk ape lives in the Florida Everglades—the largest swamp in the United States.

Some people say the skunk ape looks like this hairy dude.

He later set up the Skunk Ape Research Headquarters, a place where he and others could study the ape. Unfortunately, the only real evidence they have is stories people tell. He also started a Skunk Ape Festival that takes place each year.

People who believe the skunk ape is real claim to have seen it and smelled it. Some have photos. Some have casts of its footprints. Some even found hair. However, all of this evidence could be fake. The prints and hair could belong to another kind of animal. One skunk ape turned out to be a monkey that had escaped from a zoo.

Most people do not believe the skunk ape is real without scientific proof. Still, people disagree about whether the skunk ape is real or a hoax. It remains a mystery. ■

Vocabulary

primate: a mammal such as a human, monkey, or ape
endangered: in danger of dying out

Your Turn

Use the Skills List to fill in the chart below. Write the name of the skill described. Then, decide if the skill is helpful with what you are reading. Explain why or why not.

Skills List

- recognizing facts and opinions
- connecting across texts
- recognizing bias and viewpoint
- assessing evidence for opinions
- making generalizations
- identifying an author's purpose

Skill	Is Using This Skill Helpful with This Passage?
When you come up with a broad statement about your reading, you could be _____	☐ Yes ☐ No Why? Why not?
When you think that an author is not being fair in his or her writing, you could be _____	☐ Yes ☐ No Why? Why not?
When you can tell that a supporting idea is not a fact but someone's belief, you could be _____	☐ Yes ☐ No Why? Why not?
When you think about how ideas you read in more than one place are alike or different, you could be _____	☐ Yes ☐ No Why? Why not?

Your Choice

Circle the correct answer.

1. **The Everglades is a good place for the skunk ape because —**

   A. there is plenty of space and many people to help it.
   B. there is plenty of space and not many people to bother it.
   C. the park is in Florida.
   D. monkeys often escape into the park.

2. **A fact supporting the opinion that the skunk ape is a hoax is —**

   A. there is no scientific proof.
   B. the skunk ape is a primate.
   C. many people claim to have seen and smelled it.
   D. David Shealy found some hair.

3. **Which sentence about Connecting Across Texts is true?**

   A. More than one source for information is used.
   B. The texts must be written by the same author.
   C. The texts always show images.
   D. It is hard to find more than one text on a topic.

4. **When an animal is endangered, it —**

   A. is safe from people.
   B. lives in a swamp.
   C. might not live long.
   D. probably has a museum in Florida.

(See answers for Critical Thinking Skills, Lesson 8 to check your work.)

Number Correct:

Write Back...

How is the skill of recognizing bias or point of view different from the skill of identifying the author's purpose? Explain.

THE RABBIT AND THE TORTOISE

Reading Strategy

Stop and think about what you have read
As you read, stop and think about your reading. Underline words that tell you about the characters. Write notes beside each paragraph so you can remember each event.

Sometimes being speedy doesn't matter. Find out why.

Rabbit and Tortoise lived in the city. They liked eating out in restaurants and going to concerts. They especially loved going to basketball games.

Tortoise's love of basketball always seemed a little strange to Rabbit. Rabbit was very fast and very athletic. It made sense that he liked basketball, but Tortoise was really slow. He was not at all athletic.

"You're the slowest guy in the city," Rabbit said, teasing Tortoise. "How can someone so slow like basketball?"

"I've got **stamina**," Tortoise would always reply.

They had this argument often. It always drove Rabbit crazy. So, finally, he challenged Tortoise to a race.

"We'll start by the river and race a hundred blocks north," Rabbit said. "The first one to reach the gate of Forest Park wins. Then we'll see how great stamina is."

Rabbit easily took the lead.

Slow and steady wins the race.

Tortoise and Rabbit went down to the river, and the race began. Or, rather, it began for tortoise. After saying "Go," he charged up-town. Rabbit, on the other hand, bought a newspaper. He plopped down on a bench by the river. "This is going to be the easiest race I've ever won," he said. Finally, about an hour later, Rabbit finished the sports page. He stood up and started running. He took off at a blistering speed. About fifty blocks later, he caught up with Tortoise. "You're going to have to do better than this," Rabbit yelled, and kept on running.

Rabbit ran another fifty blocks, to the edge of Forest Park. He could see the main gate–it was about thirty feet away. Instead of crossing the finish line, he found a spot under a shady tree. "I think I'll take a little nap," he said, laughing. "I've got all day."

Rabbit quickly fell asleep. He probably would have slept all afternoon if something hadn't suddenly woken him up. At first he was a little confused. Finally, he sat up and looked around. There was tortoise, about three feet from the gate. He was calling out to Rabbit.

Rabbit quickly jumped up. He **sprinted** towards the finish line, but it was too late. Tortoise touched the gate with his pointy green nose.

"I won," Tortoise yelled.

"No way," Rabbit said, "I'm fifty times faster than you."

"You're fifty times faster," Tortoise said, "but I'm **persistent**. And you can't beat that." ■

Vocabulary

stamina: the drive to keep going
sprinted: ran fast
persistent: lasting, determined

9 Analyzing Character Traits

Your Turn

Reread "The Rabbit and the Tortoise." Think about Rabbit. Fill in information about what he says, does and thinks. Then, use his words and actions to decide on his character traits.

The character —

says

does

thinks

Rabbit

Character Traits
How would you describe this character?

Clue
Use examples of what the character says, does, and thinks to decide on character traits.

Clue
Look at the character's relationships with other characters.

Your Choice

Circle the correct answer.

① Why does Rabbit challenge Tortoise to a race?

A. He wants to prove that speed is better than stamina.
B. He wants to prove that he is stronger than Tortoise.
C. He wants to help Tortoise run faster.
D. He wants to train for basketball camp.

② Which of Rabbit's character traits leads to his failure?

A. He's fast.
B. He's athletic.
C. He's proud.
D. He's carefree.

③ Which character trait helps Tortoise win the race?

A. He's fast.
B. He's slow.
C. He's persistent.
D. He's friendly.

④ How can stamina be more important than speed?

A. It makes you faster.
B. It makes you stronger.
C. It keeps you cool.
D. It keeps you going.

(See answers for Critical Thinking Skills, Lesson 9 to check your work.)

Number Correct:

Write Back...

Why are character traits important in this story?

Analyzing Conflict and Resolution

Your Turn

Reread "The Rabbit and the Tortoise." What is Tortoise's problem? How does he solve it?

Conflict (Problem)

Resolution (How the Problem Is Solved)

Your Choice

Circle the correct answer.

1 **Why doesn't Rabbit keep running from the beginning to the end of the race?**

A. He gets tired and needs a break.
B. He is sure he will win easily.
C. He wants Tortoise to win.
D. He doesn't like to run races.

2 **What is the story's main conflict?**

A. Tortoise is angry at himself for not running faster.
B. Rabbit is tired of Tortoise's bragging.
C. Tortoise keeps winning races against Rabbit.
D. Rabbit is sick of hearing that stamina is great.

3 **In the story's resolution, Tortoise proves that —**

A. the quickest one always wins.
B. Rabbit planned to cheat.
C. stamina can win the race.
D. he is fifty times faster than Rabbit.

4 **How do you know that Tortoise is persistent?**

A. He keeps going.
B. He runs slowly.
C. He wins the race easily.
D. He lets Rabbit win the race.

(See answers for Critical Thinking Skills, Lesson 10 to check your work.)

Number Correct:

Write Back...

How does understanding conflict and resolution help you understand the characters in a story?

My Week with Chicken Pox

**What's worse than getting really sick?
How about getting really sick on vacation.**

Reading Strategy

Make Connections
As you read, ask yourself "What does this remind me of in my life?" Your knowledge can help you understand what you are reading.

We weren't even there yet, but I could already smell salt in the air. My family has taken the same vacation since I was little. I couldn't wait to feel the warm sand under my feet. This year I was going to check out the tide pools.

We got there in the afternoon. I started to put on my swimsuit, but I didn't feel too well. In fact, I didn't feel like swimming at all. By the time all my cousins showed up, I was completely sick.

"I'm sorry, Elena," the doctor said. "You have chicken pox."

The doctor said I'd have chicken pox for the entire week!

Sometimes chicken pox isn't that bad. In my case, however, I thought I was going to die. I itched like crazy. My stomach hurt. I had terrible headaches. I had a raging fever. It was really rough. Still, there was one good thing that happened during all of it.

Elena lay miserably in bed while her cousins hit the waves.

Elena was surprised to find that needlepoint isn't all that boring.

I have this aunt that I've never really been that close to. She's my mother's sister, and, honestly, I've never thought she liked me very much. I can be a little loud, and a little "**rambunctious**," as my mother puts it. My aunt is quiet, and not exactly active. Last year she sat in the same chair for the entire vacation, reading books. This year, when I was sick, for some reason she took a real interest in me. She was the one who brought me my medicine. She helped me put on the disgusting cream that helped stop the itching.

She also taught me how to needlepoint, which is something I never thought I'd like. She gave me a pattern for a belt and showed me how to make different kinds of stitches and knots. If I hadn't done it myself, I'd say it sounded pretty boring. I made a belt, though. And it was a great **distraction** from all the itching.

It's funny how this kind of thing works. My aunt wasn't exactly the person I thought I'd hang out with at the beach. While I can't say I had a good time, it was really great to get to know my aunt. As for the needlepoint, I'm not sure if it's going to take the place of softball and chilling at the mall. Still, I liked it, and I'm making a cool book cover. So I think I'll keep doing it for a while. ∎

Analyzing Mood

Your Turn

Read "My Week with Chicken Pox" again. Fill in the boxes with examples from the story that tell where and when the story takes place and how the characters feel. Then, think about how you feel. This information will help you find the mood, or the feeling created by the story.

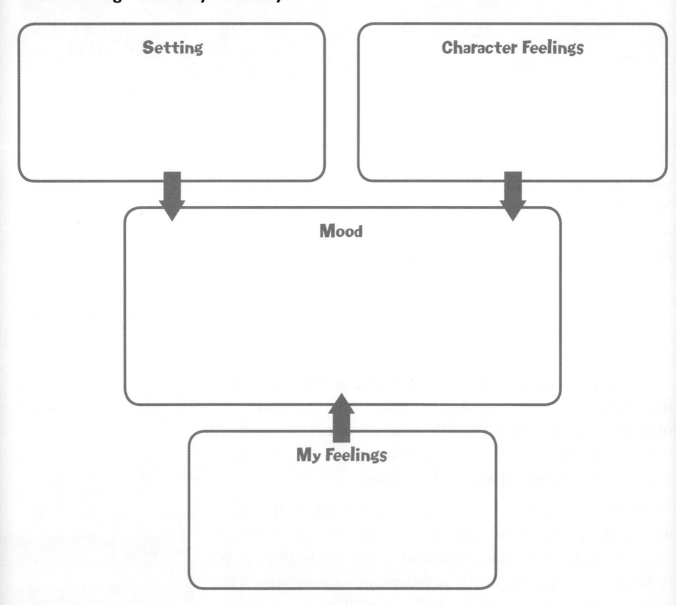

Setting

Character Feelings

Mood

My Feelings

Your Choice

Circle the correct answer.

1 **During the week, Elena learned —**

    A. all about tide pools.

    B. who her aunt was.

    C. to needlepoint.

    D. how to chill at the mall.

2 **Which word best describes the mood in the first paragraph?**

    A. gloomy

    B. entertaining

    C. peaceful

    D. cheerful

3 **When Elena finds out she has chicken pox, the story's mood becomes —**

    A. angry.

    B. funny.

    C. gloomy.

    D. lively.

4 **Which of the following children might be described as rambunctious?**

    A. a girl spinning in circles and yelling

    B. a boy reading a book

    C. a girl bicycling in a park

    D. a boy hiking up a tall mountain

(See answers for Critical Thinking Skills, Lesson 11 to check your work.)

Number Correct:

Write Back...

How did the setting affect the mood of the story? Would having chicken pox be as bad if Elena weren't on her vacation?

Drawing Conclusions

Your Turn

Read the clues from the story. Then, think about the story. From the clues, what can you conclude about how Elena's feelings about her aunt changed by the end of the story? Write your conclusion in the box.

Clue from the Story

I've never thought she liked me much.

Your Conclusion

Clue from the Story

For some reason she took a real interest in me. She was the one who brought me my medicine. She helped me put on the disgusting cream.

Clue from the Story

My aunt wasn't exactly the person I thought I'd hang out with at the beach. While I can't say I had a good time, it was really great to get to know my aunt.

Your Choice

Circle the correct answer.

1. **Why didn't Elena spend time swimming at the beach?**

   A. She wanted to needlepoint a belt.
   B. She was sick with chicken pox.
   C. She preferred being with her aunt.
   D. She wanted to chill at the mall.

2. **From what you know about Elena's aunt, you can conclude that she would enjoy —**

   A. listening to music.
   B. racing bikes.
   C. surfing.
   D. singing.

3. **What can you conclude about Elena's opinion of needlepoint at the end of the story?**

   A. She thinks it is boring.
   B. She doesn't want to do it again.
   C. She likes it and will continue.
   D. She feels forced to do it.

4. **Which of the following is most likely to be a distraction from homework?**

   A. studying for a test
   B. writing a research paper
   C. writing an essay
   D. watching television

(See answers for Critical Thinking Skills, Lesson 12 to check your work.)

Number Correct:

Write Back...

How can drawing conclusions help you?

MAKING A DIFFERENCE

Comprehension Skills

You Have Already Learned

- Analyzing Character Traits
- Analyzing Conflict and Resolution
- Analyzing Mood
- Drawing Conclusions

What difference can a good coach make?

The sign practically called out to me: BOXING TRYOUTS SEPTEMBER 6. "That's it!" I thought to myself. "That's what I want to do." I decided to train during the summer. Then I'd be ready for tryouts in the fall. When I got home, I pulled out my dad's old punching bag and boxing gloves. After a few punches and a bit of bobbing around, I realized that I needed a trainer. I decided to head for the gym.

The smell of leather and sweat rushed at me as I opened the door to the gym. As I watched the fighters trade punches, I thought "These guys are good!" After a while I worked up the nerve to talk with one of the boxers.

"Will you be my coach for the summer?" I asked.

"No, man. I'm already coaching another kid," he answered.

I asked three other guys. "No," "No," and "No." I was about to give up when a tall man with huge muscles approached me. "What's your name, kid?" he asked.

I needed some help from a coach.

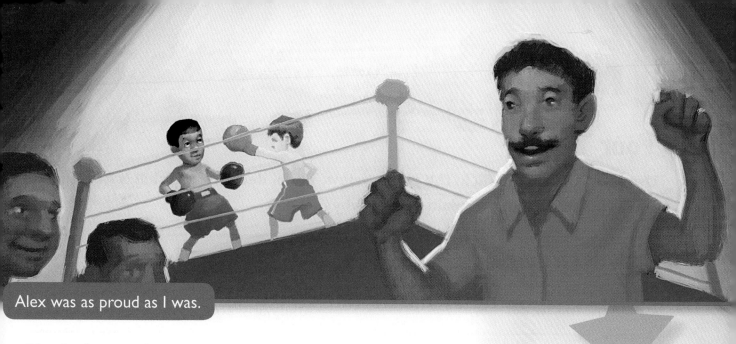
Alex was as proud as I was.

I looked up at the muscle man before me. "Tyrone," I answered.

"Would you like to train with me, Tyrone?" He introduced himself as Alex Duran. I nearly fell over when he told me about the championships he had won.

Everyday after warming up, Alex took me into the boxing ring and taught me how to throw a good punch. I felt like a failure in the ring because I kept getting hit. I didn't know how to block the punches.

"Alex, you don't want to waste your time on me. I'm not getting any better," Alex looked disappointed, "You, Tyrone, are a winner, and winners do not quit."

I used Alex's words as an **incentive** to keep training. Soon, I was bobbing up and down and weaving left and right like a pro. Other boxers started cheering me on, and Alex proudly took a bow—as if he were the one making the moves.

After I made the school team, I ran to the gym to tell the other fighters. Somehow the guys already knew and had set up a party for me. As I walked around, the guys socked me playfully and slapped me on the back. This time the punches felt great. Alex told me that the hard work had made the difference. I said, "No, Alex. You made the difference." ∎

Vocabulary

incentive: a reason to continue

Your Turn

Use the Skills List to fill in the chart below. Then, decide if the skill is helpful with what you are reading. Explain why or why not.

Skills List
- drawing conclusions
- analyzing mood
- analyzing character traits
- analyzing conflict and resolution

Skill	Is Using This Skill Helpful with This Passage?
When you use clues in a story to form your own ideas, you could be _____	☐ Yes ☐ No Why? Why not?
When you figure out what kind of a person a character is, you could be _____	☐ Yes ☐ No Why? Why not?
When you think about how a story's setting makes you feel, you are _____	☐ Yes ☐ No Why? Why not?
When you think about problems and how characters solve those problems, you are _____	☐ Yes ☐ No Why? Why not?

Your Choice

Circle the best answer.

1 **How did Tyrone become a good boxer?**

  A. He was born that way.
  B. He joined the school team.
  C. He used his dad's old equipment.
  D. He got Alex Duran's help.

2 **What can you conclude about the other fighters at the gym?**

  A. They don't like Tyrone.
  B. They don't notice Tyrone.
  C. They think of Tyrone as a friend.
  D. They think Tyrone is a coward.

3 **Which character trait best describes Alex Duran?**

  A. honest
  B. humble
  C. foolish
  D. generous

4 **An incentive can make you —**

  A. feel uncomfortable.
  B. want to try harder.
  C. feel like a pro.
  D. want to quit.

(See answers for Critical Thinking Skills, Lesson 13 to check your work.)

Number Correct:

Write Back...

Describe an ordinary hero you know. Give the character traits of your hero.

Making the World a Better Place

Better Place

Can kindness really make a difference?

Comprehension Skills

- **Lesson 14:** Interpreting Figurative Language
- **Lesson 15:** Identifying Genre

Reading Strategy

Picture in Your Mind
As you read, notice how the author helps you form pictures in your mind.

The Good Deed Day

'What did I do?' I cannot say.
The day passed by so quick.
But here I stand, with filthy clothes.
A tow'r of mud so thick.

First, Nate was ill. He was so sad
That Jasper said to me,
"What can we do to make this bad
Leave Nate like one-two-three?"

So off we went to find a gift
That did not cost a lot.
We made a card with many jokes.
We did it on the spot.

Nate laughed and laughed.
He was as pleased as pigs in warm, wet mud.
It made us grin; it made us smile.
But then, we heard a thud!

Nate's mom let out an awful **shriek.**
We ran to give her **aid**.
What did we find when we got there?
She'd spilled the lemonade.

Dirt washes off, but kindness stays.

We helped her clean.
She thanked us both and asked us if we would
Help her to hang her wet, clean clothes.
We said that sure, we could.

The neighbor's dog was zooming by.
He'd gotten loose and free.
The next we knew, the clothes were down
And pup was right on me!

First went the dog back to his house.
The neighbor was so glad.
Then back we went to wash the clothes.
We weren't very mad.

When clothes were washed and on the line,
We had to bid goodbye.
We both went home with happy hearts.
And so the day passed by.

A tiny woman with a huge heart!

What a Woman!

When Mother Teresa saw people living on the streets, she knew she must do something. She opened a school to teach them to read and write. She then found other ways to help, too.

Working as hard as a beaver, she started a hospice. There sick people got food, care, and comfort.

This worker bee did not stop there. She saved thirty-seven children trapped in a war area. She also sold her car to help sick people in Africa.

Although she died in 1997, her work will go on. The world smiles each day because of her! ■

Vocabulary

aid: help
shriek: a yell

Interpreting Figurative Language

Your Turn

Reread "Making the World a Better Place." Find two examples of figurative language. Determine what type of figurative language they are. Then, tell what they mean and why the author used them.

Figurative Language	Literal Meaning	Why the Author Used Figurative Language
☐ metaphor ☐ simile ☐ personification	The sentence means —	The author wanted —
☐ metaphor ☐ simile ☐ personification	The sentence means —	The author wanted —

Your Choice

Circle the correct answer.

1 **How did Mother Teresa raise money to help people in Africa?**

  A. She started a school.

  B. She sold her school.

  C. She sold her car.

  D. She washed people's clothes.

2 **What sentence tells how quickly the boys in "The Good Deed Day," want their friend to get well?**

  A. Nate was ill. He was so sad.

  B. This bad must leave Nate like one-two-three.

  C. Nate was as pleased as pigs in warm, wet mud.

  D. He'd gotten loose and free.

3 **Why does the author call Mother Teresa a worker bee?**

  A. She worked extremely hard.

  B. She did not live like a queen bee.

  C. She gave honey to the poor.

  D. She worked in India.

4 **How did Mother Teresa come to the aid of the sick?**

  A. She saved children in war.

  B. She opened a hospice.

  C. She built a school.

  D. She moved to India.

(See answers for Critical Thinking Skills, Lesson 14 to check your work.)

Number Correct:

Write Back...

Describe a person who has done a good deed for you. Use a simile or a metaphor in your description.

Lesson 15 · Identifying Genre

Your Turn

"The Good Deed Day" and "What a Woman!" are examples of two different genres. Use the flow chart below to find each genre.

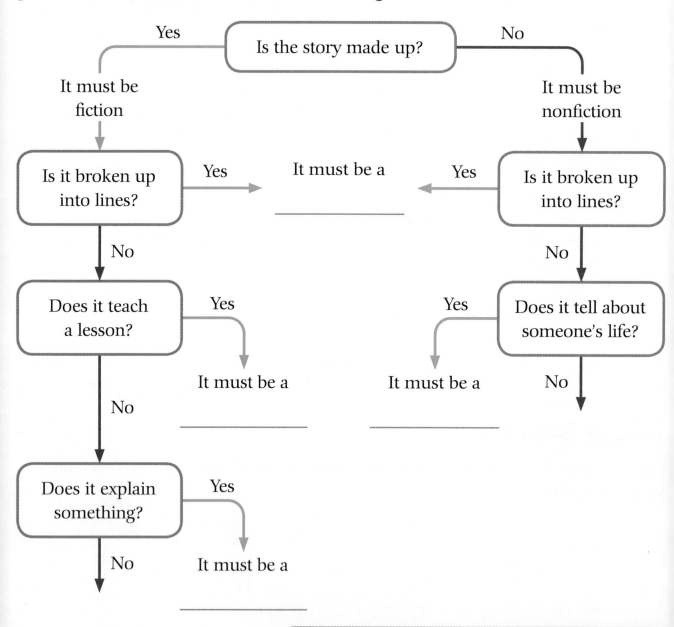

Yes — Is the story made up? — No

It must be fiction

It must be nonfiction

Is it broken up into lines? — Yes → It must be a _____ ← Yes — Is it broken up into lines?

No

No

Does it teach a lesson? — Yes → It must be a _____

Yes → It must be a _____ — Does it tell about someone's life? — No

No

Does it explain something? — Yes → It must be a _____

No

"The Good Deed Day" is a _____.

"What a Woman!" is a _____.

Your Choice

Circle the correct answer.

1. **In "The Good Deed Day," how did the narrator feel at the end of the day?**

   A. tired
   B. happy
   C. mad
   D. sick

2. **What genre is "The Good Deed Day"?**

   A. poem
   B. myth
   C. biography
   D. fable

3. **How can you tell the genre of "What a Woman"?**

   A. It is a made up story.
   B. It is a true story.
   C. It was written in a special format.
   D. It rhymes.

4. **A person would most likely shriek when coming across which animal?**

   A. a cat
   B. a snake
   C. a bird
   D. a dog

(See answers for Critical Thinking Skills, Lesson 15 to check your work.)

Number Correct:

Write Back...

Write a short biography about someone who has been kind to you.

TRASH IN SPACE

There's more in outer space than you think.

When you look up at the night sky, you probably expect to see the moon, stars, or even planets. Asteroids, comets, and meteors are flying around, too. There's a lot more floating around up there, though. Most of it is natural such as rocks and dust. However, there's a whole lot of trash, too—and some of the pieces are as large as trucks.

This trash can travel as fast as 18,000 miles an hour, making even the smallest piece of trash extremely dangerous. How? Just think about dropping a dime while you walk down the street. It hardly makes a sound when it falls on the ground. If you drop the same dime from a skyscraper, it builds speed as it falls. That dime could put a dent, or even a hole, in the roof of a car. Now, picture that same dime traveling in space at 18,000 miles an hour. It could slam into the space shuttle with the force of a bomb! Luckily that hasn't happened, but tiny flecks of old paint have been known to chip the windows of space shuttles.

NASA is well aware of the problem. One NASA scientist, Nicholas Johnson, tracks more than 13,000 pieces of space trash. He makes sure space shuttles and satellites stay clear of most space **debris**.

Comprehension Skills

- **Lesson 16:** Making Judgments
- **Lesson 17:** Summarizing

Reading Strategy

Use Background Knowledge

You already know something about much of what you read. Good readers combine what they know with new information.

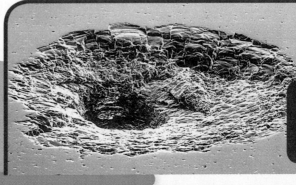

A tiny paint chip put this hole in the window of a space shuttle.

The International Space Station could be badly damaged by space junk.

How Did The Trash Get There?

The first satellite was launched into space in 1957. Since then people have sent more than 4,000 satellites into space. Some satellites do not find their way home; they orbit the earth for years. They become space trash. One astronaut lost his camera while he was taking pictures from space. Another astronaut lost his glove. Both items are now space trash, and they might be whizzing around the Earth to this day.

Falling Space Junk?

Space trash isn't much of a problem if it is far out in deep space. Items that **orbit** Earth from more than 600 miles away can continue circling for more than a century. However, the trash that is closer to Earth just might enter the Earth's atmosphere. If it does, most of it will burn; **gravity** will pull the rest of it down to Earth. This happened in 1979 when the 150-ton Skylab fell out of the sky. No one was hurt, though. Most of it landed in the ocean.

If you're worried that space trash will land on you, think again. Here is one case in which what goes up does not

FUN FACTS

- The oldest piece of space junk is the Vanguard I. It has been orbiting since 1958.

- Twenty tons of space junk are parked on the moon.

Vocabulary

debris: fragments of broken trash
orbit: to travel along a path around the Earth
gravity: the force that pulls items to Earth

16 Making Judgments

Your Turn

Read "Trash in Space" again. What did you think of the Web site article? Circle your rating on the scale below. Then, write the evidence that matches your rating.

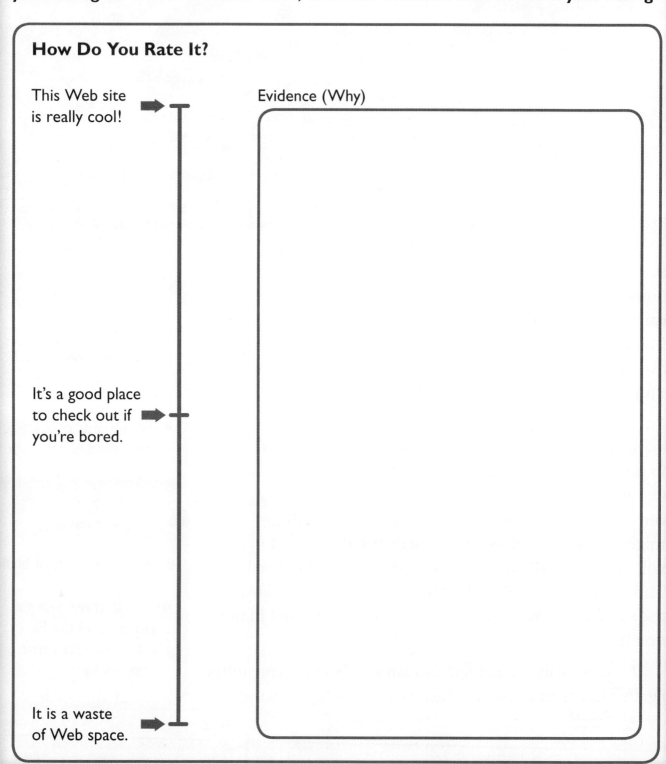

How Do You Rate It?

This Web site is really cool!

Evidence (Why)

It's a good place to check out if you're bored.

It is a waste of Web space.

Your Choice

Circle the correct answer.

1 **Space garbage can be dangerous because it —**

   A. is always extremely large.
   B. can travel really fast.
   C. usually falls on people.
   D. always burns up as it falls.

2 **When you make a judgment, you need to understand —**

   A. genres and conflicts.
   B. characters and setting.
   C. opinions and reasons.
   D. metaphors and conclusions.

3 **Which of the following is a judgment?**

   A. Trash is circling Earth.
   B. Space trash travels fast.
   C. Space trash is a big problem.
   D. An astronaut lost his camera.

4 **"Satellites must stay clear of debris." In this sentence, *debris* means —**

   A. Earth.
   B. trash.
   C. shuttles.
   D. asteroids.

(See answers for Critical Thinking Skills, Lesson 16 to check your work.)

Number Correct:

Write Back...

Why is it important to make judgments about information you read on the Web?

Your Turn

Reread "Trash in Space." Then, write information from each paragraph in the boxes below. Use the information in the boxes to write a summary of the passage.

Paragraph I

This paragraph is about

The most important ideas are

+

Paragraphs 2 and 3

These paragraphs are about

The most important ideas are

+

=

Paragraph 4

This paragraph is about

The most important ideas are

+

Paragraph 5

This paragraph is about

The most important ideas are

Summary

The passage is about

Your Choice

Circle the correct answer.

1 Why is there trash in space?

A. The wind blew it there.

B. It blew off other planets.

C. People sent it there to avoid filling landfills.

D. It was lost during past space missions.

2 To write a summary you need to know —

A. the important information in an article.

B. how to make a good judgment.

C. how to support your opinions with evidence.

D. the questions you would ask about an article.

3 Which of these statements summarizes the problem presented in the passage?

A. Most space trash falls to Earth.

B. Countries launch old satellites.

C. Outer space is full of trash.

D. Satellites stop working.

4 "Many objects orbit Earth." This sentence means —

A. many objects blow off of Earth.

B. many objects travel around Earth.

C. many objects fall to Earth.

D. many objects are on Earth.

(See answers for Critical Thinking Skills, Lesson 17 to check your work.)

Number Correct:

Write Back...

What is the benefit of summarizing articles you have read?

SPORTS AGENT TO THE STARS

Help make the next great athlete a star.

Sports stars are more than just athletes. You see them on TV and in magazines. They have million-dollar **contracts**. Most professional athletes don't get those contracts themselves. A sports agent sets up deals between athletes and team owners. Deals are also made by agents for sports stars to advertise products. These **endorsements** bring in more money if the player will advertise things like sneakers or sport drinks.

In years past, the goal of a sports agent was to get an athlete a good contract with a team. In the 1960s that all changed with television. Suddenly athletes became stars. One man who helped changed the business was Mark McCormack. He's best known for putting world-famous golfer Arnold Palmer on TV. McCormack became one of

Many professional athletes such as Derek Jeter and Tiger Woods have sports agents.

Leigh Steinberg's clients claim that he is a smart sports agent with a heart of gold.

the most powerful agents in sports by making good deals for his **clients**. His clients have included big-name sports figures like Tiger Woods and Derek Jeter.

Sports agents used to work behind the scenes and people knew little about them, but in the 1990s a popular movie showed viewers what sports agents do. The movie showed two sides of the business. On one side is the agent who is only out to get as much money as possible for clients. On the other side is the agent who is looking out for his client's overall best interests, not just in the area of money.

The main character in that movie was based on sports agent, Leigh Steinberg. He has gotten over $2 billion in contracts for his clients. Steinberg is a smart businessman with a heart of gold. He's not out only to get the most money for clients. He also wants his clients to be good role models. Steinberg asks his clients to give back to the community. The idea is working. Steinberg's clients have donated more than $50 million to charities!

If you love sports and have a good sense for business, becoming a sports agent might be the career for you. You'll have to decide on which kind of agent you will be. Will you use your career to help people? Or, will you just go for the money? ■

Review

Your Turn

Use the Skills List to fill in the chart below. Then, decide if the skill is helpful with what you are reading. Explain why or why not.

Skills List

- recognizing facts and opinions
- assessing evidence for opinions
- making generalizations
- connecting across texts
- recognizing bias and viewpoint
- identifying author's purpose
- analyzing character traits
- analyzing conflict and resolution
- analyzing mood
- drawing conclusions
- interpreting figurative language
- identifying genre
- making judgments
- summarizing

Skill	Is Using This Skill Helpful with This Passage?
When you figure out how an author uses language to mean something different from its literal meaning, you could be _____	☐ Yes ☐ No Why? Why not?
When you decide what you think about something you are reading, you could be _____	☐ Yes ☐ No Why? Why not?
When you retell the main ideas of something you have read, you could be _____	☐ Yes ☐ No Why? Why not?
When you tell some general things about the main idea and characters in a story, you could be _____	☐ Yes ☐ No Why? Why not?

Your Choice

Circle the correct answer.

1 A sports agent —

  A. sets up practice for athletes.
  B. plays on the team with clients.
  C. sets up contracts for clients.
  D. is not helpful with endorsements.

2 A "heart of gold" is a metaphor for what?

  A. loving money
  B. being kind-hearted
  C. being cold-hearted
  D. loving jewelry

3 Which is a good generalization about all sports agents?

  A. Sports agents are just out for the money.
  B. Sports agents work for the good of the community.
  C. Sports agents set up contracts between athletes and teams.
  D. Sports agents have lots of money.

4 Endorsements show that someone —

  A. learns about or studies something.
  B. gives away or donates something.
  C. makes or creates something.
  D. approves or supports something.

(See answers for Critical Thinking Skills, Lesson 18 to check your work.)

Number Correct:

Write Back...

What critical thinking skills would you use for this type of career?

Independent Reading Record

Use the graphic organizers from pages 63–79 to practice these Critical Thinking skills with the other books you read.

Skill	Title of Book and Pages
Recognizing Facts and Opinions	
Assessing Evidence for Opinions	
Making Generalizations	
Connecting Across Texts	
Recognizing Bias and Viewpoint	
Identifying an Author's Purpose	
Analyzing Character Traits	
Analyzing Conflict and Resolution	
Analyzing Mood	
Drawing Conclusions	
Interpreting Figurative Language	
Identifying Genre	
Making Judgments	
Summarizing	
Review Critical Thinking Skills	

Recognizing Facts and Opinions

Look for facts and opinions. Then, write them into the chart below.

Facts (statements you can prove)	Opinions (feelings and beliefs)

Assessing Evidence for Opinions

Find an opinion stated by the writer. Write this opinion below in the top box. Write reasons the writer has this opinion in the next boxes. Then, fill in evidence from the passage that states facts supporting the opinion.

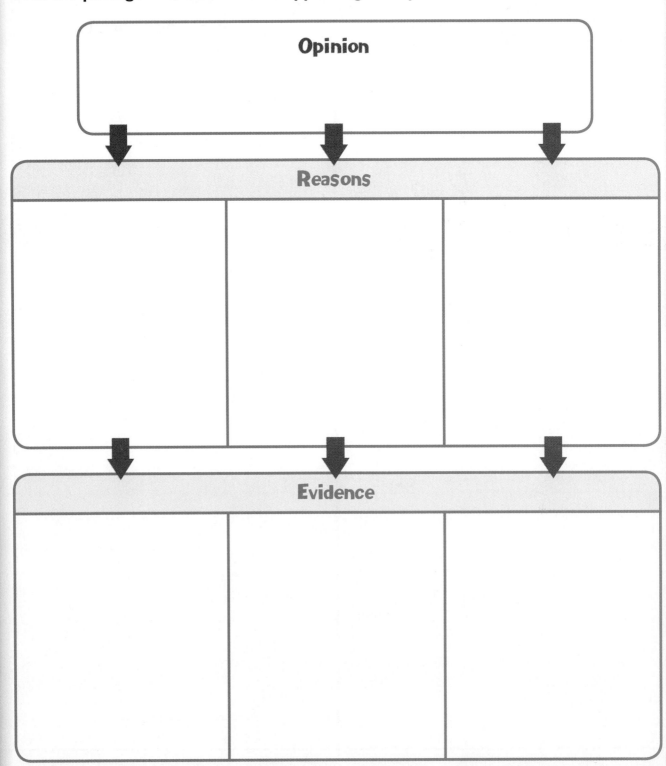

Opinion

Reasons

Evidence

Making Generalizations

Look for related ideas to make a generalization.

Topic
Some examples say
Other examples say

↓

Generalization
(A general idea that might be true in a lot of cases.)

Connecting Across Texts

Write details that both texts share in the space shared by both boxes. Write details that are different into the boxes under each title.

Text #1 Title: _____

Details Both Texts Share

Text #2 Title: _____

Recognizing Bias and Point of View

Think about the writer's feelings or opinions about the subject you are reading about. Fill in the graphic organizer below with the writer's words showing positive (good) and negative (bad) opinions about the subject. Sometimes you can tell the author's bias by which side of the graphic organizer has more evidence.

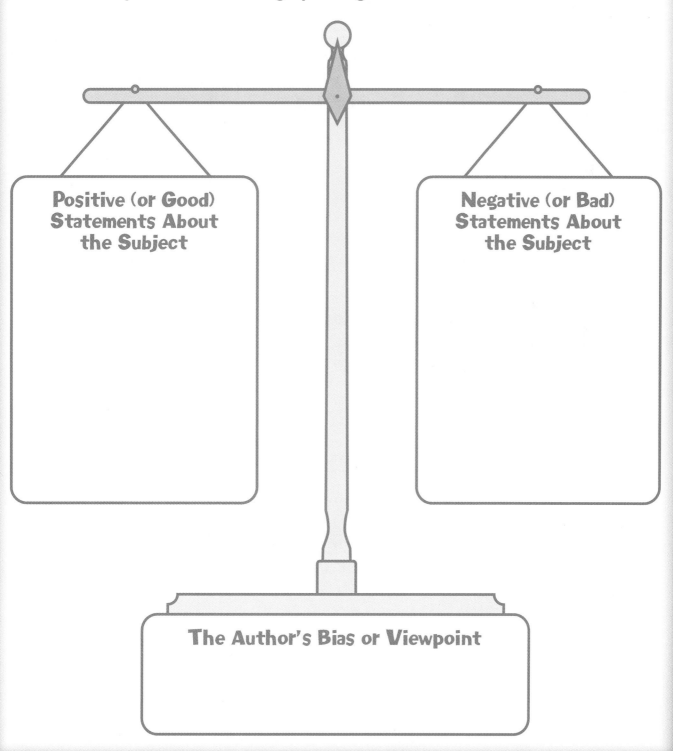

Positive (or Good) Statements About the Subject

Negative (or Bad) Statements About the Subject

The Author's Bias or Viewpoint

Identifying an Author's Purpose

Authors have different purposes for writing. Look at the details the writer gives. Add them to the graphic organizer below. What do you think is the author's purpose?

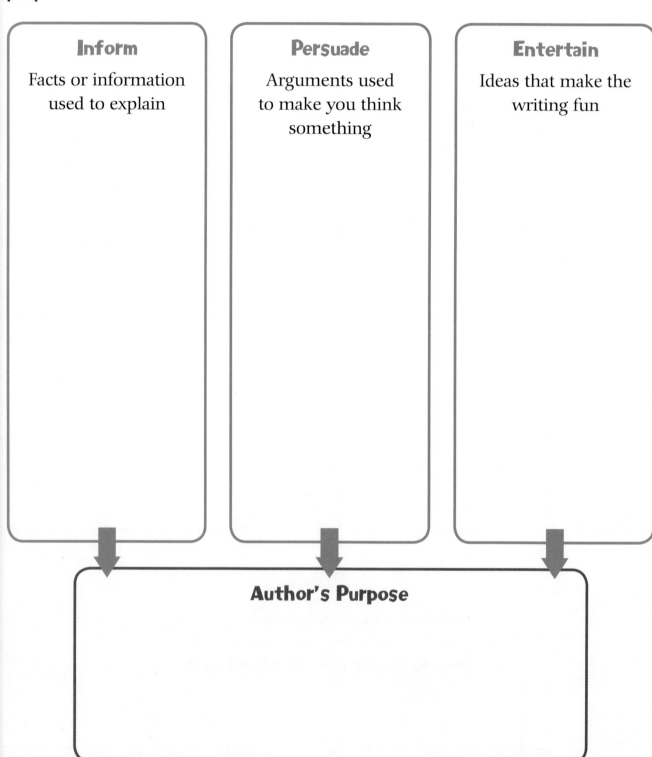

Inform

Facts or information used to explain

Persuade

Arguments used to make you think something

Entertain

Ideas that make the writing fun

Author's Purpose

Use the **Skills List** to fill in the chart. Then, decide if the skill is helpful with what you are reading. Explain why or why not.

Skills List
- recognizing facts and opinions
- connecting across texts
- recognizing bias and viewpoint
- assessing evidence for opinions
- making generalizations
- identifying an author's purpose

Skill	Is Using This Skill Helpful with This Passage?
When you determine if a writer uses valid facts to support an opinion, you could be _____	☐ Yes ☐ No Why? Why not?
When you look for ideas that are alike or different, you could be _____	☐ Yes ☐ No Why? Why not?
When you see that an author is using loaded language to make a point, you could be _____	☐ Yes ☐ No Why? Why not?
When you develop a broad statement about your reading, you could be _____	☐ Yes ☐ No Why? Why not?
When you figure out why an author wrote a passage, you could be _____	☐ Yes ☐ No Why? Why not?
When you look for what can be proven and what is personal belief, you could be _____	☐ Yes ☐ No Why? Why not?

Analyzing Character Traits

Choose an important character in a story. Then, use clues in the story to fill in the two boxes.

The character —

says

does

thinks

Character Name:

_____

Character Traits

How would you describe this character?

Clue
Use examples of what the character says, does, and thinks to decide on character traits.

Clue
Look at the character's relationships with other characters.

Analyzing Conflict and Resolution

Fill in the top box with details about the problem in a story. Some characters have conflicts with other characters. Some struggle with nature. Others struggle with their own feelings or fears. How a character solves the problem is the resolution. Tell how the problem is solved in the bottom box.

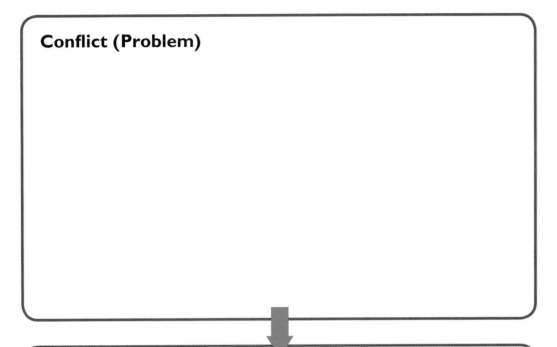

Conflict (Problem)

Resolution (How the Problem Is Solved)

Lesson 11 Analyzing Mood

Fill in the boxes with examples from the story that tell you where and when the story takes place and how the characters feel. Then, think about how you feel. Fill in the Mood box with information about the mood, or feeling created by the story.

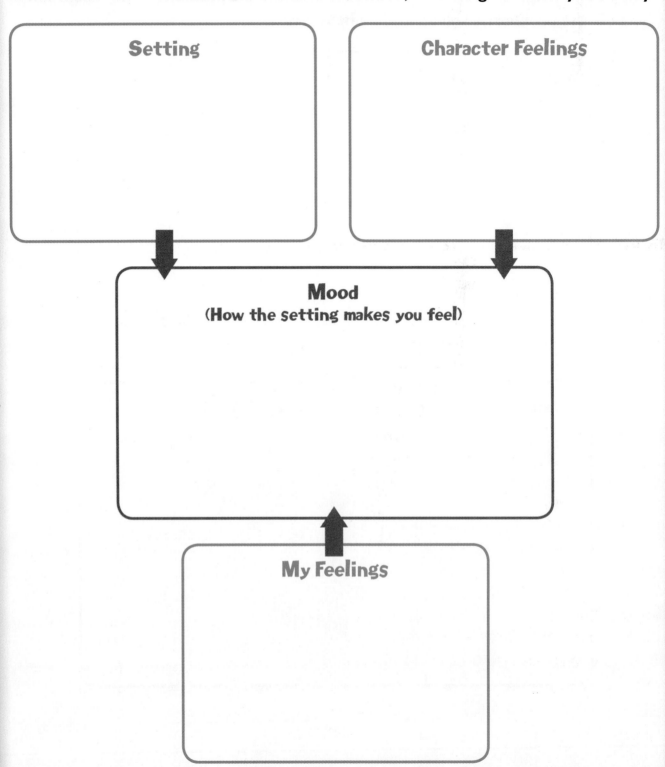

Setting

Character Feelings

Mood
(How the setting makes you feel)

My Feelings

2 Drawing Conclusions

An author doesn't always tell readers everything in a story. Sometimes the reader has to figure out parts of a story.

Write clues from the story in the first three boxes. Then, write your conclusion based on those clues into the box on the right.

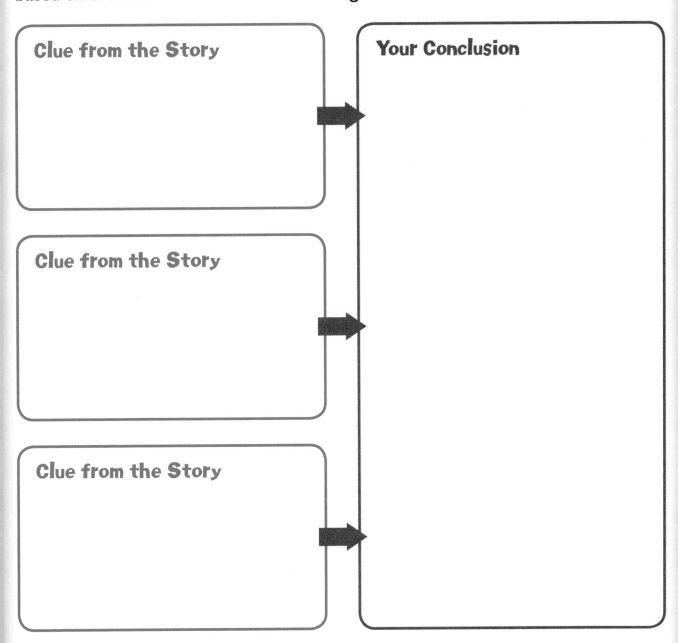

Clue from the Story

Your Conclusion

Clue from the Story

Clue from the Story

Review

Use the Skills List to fill in the chart. Then, decide if the skill is helpful with what you are reading. Explain why or why not.

Skills List
- drawing conclusions
- analyzing mood
- analyzing a character's traits
- analyzing conflict and resolution

Skill	Is Using This Skill Helpful with This Passage?	
When you think about problems and how characters solve those problems, you could be _____	☐ Yes Why?	☐ No Why not?
When you describe a character based on actions and words, you could be _____	☐ Yes Why?	☐ No Why not?
When you think about how a story's setting makes you feel, you could be _____	☐ Yes Why?	☐ No Why not?
When you use clues in a passage to make your own statement, you could be _____	☐ Yes Why?	☐ No Why not?

Lesson 4: Interpreting Figurative Language

Give examples of similes, metaphors, and personification. Then, describe their meaning.

Figurative Language	Examples	Meaning
simile a comparison using "LIKE" or "AS."		
metaphor a comparison that says one thing IS another.		
personification a comparison that makes a thing or animal seem human.		

15 Identifying Genre

When you look for the genre of a piece of writing, use this flow chart. First determine if the writing is fiction or nonfiction. Then, figure out if it is a poem, a myth, a fable, or a biography.

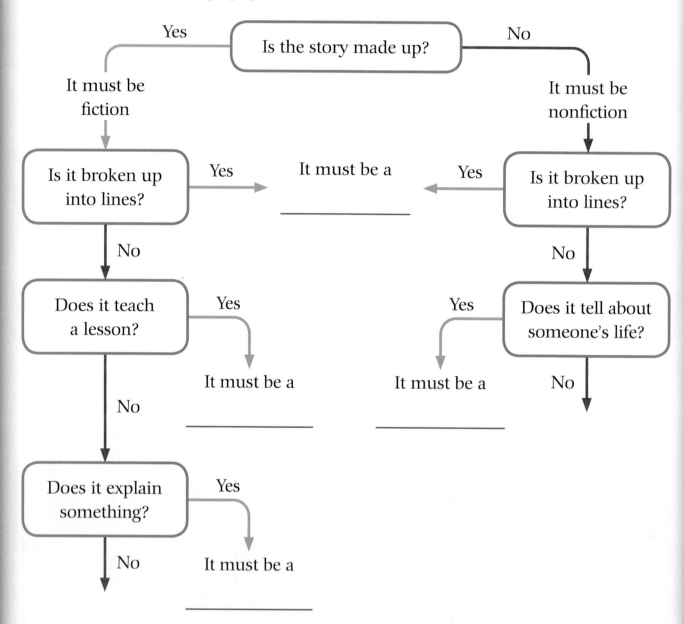

Making Judgments

Put an **X** on the line to show your opinion of the article you are reading. Then, write the evidence that matches your rating.

How Do You Rate It?

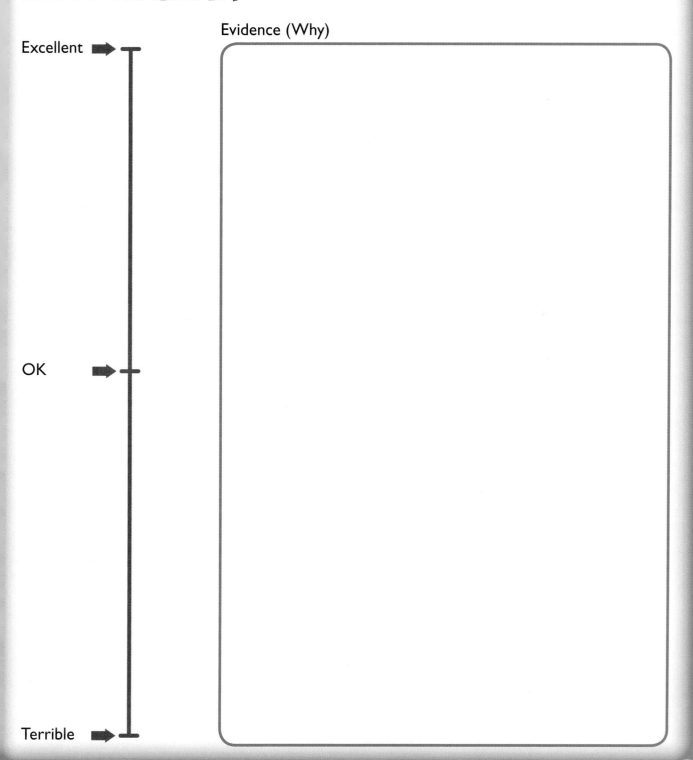

Evidence (Why)

Excellent

OK

Terrible

Summarizing

Write information from each paragraph or section in the boxes below. Use the information in the boxes to write a summary of the article. Add more boxes if you need them.

Paragraph or Section 1

This section is about

The most important ideas are that

+

Paragraph or Section 2

This section is about

The most important ideas are that

+

Paragraph or Section 3

This section is about

The most important ideas are that

=

Summary

The article is about

8 Review

Use the Skills List to fill in the chart. Then, decide if the skill is helpful with what you are reading. Explain why or why not.

Skills List

- recognizing facts and opinions
- assessing evidence for opinions
- making generalizations
- connecting across texts
- recognizing bias and viewpoint
- identifying an author's purpose
- analyzing character traits
- analyzing conflict and resolution
- analyzing mood
- drawing conclusions
- interpreting figurative language
- identifying genre
- making judgments
- summarizing

Skill	Is Using This Skill Helpful with This Passage?
When you figure out how an author uses language to mean something different from its literal meaning, you could be _____	☐ Yes ☐ No Why? Why not?
When you tell what kind of literature something is, you could be _____	☐ Yes ☐ No Why? Why not?
When you decide what you think about something you are reading, you could be _____	☐ Yes ☐ No Why? Why not?
When you retell the main points of something you have read, you could be _____	☐ Yes ☐ No Why? Why not?